GOOGLE

CLASSROOM

The Effective Practical System to Rapidly Implement and Innovate your Remote Digital Teaching Skills and be a Brilliant Model for your Students, receiving the Deserved Awards

JENNIFER CAGE

© Copyright 2020 - All rights reserved.

Table of Contents

Introduction

In the last decade, the massive spread of new technologies has revolutionized the techniques and methods of knowledge and learning transmission. With online learning (or e-learning), more and more people have the opportunity to access information and data in real-time. E-learning is one of the main tools for promoting lifelong learning—the lifelong learning that the international community has chosen as a common objective to foster creativity, competitiveness, employability, and social-economic development. E-learning is not just limited to school education, but is also aimed at adults, teachers and is often used in public administrations and companies.

"Online learning" is a self-explanatory term: learning that takes place online. This means that someone (usually a teacher or instructor) creates the content for learning and then shares it with a group of students, who can access it using internet-connection. Exams are also held online, using online exam software. You can access the content anytime, anywhere. Time and space don't matter much here. Students do not have to be in the same physical place to receive the same education. On the contrary, traditional learning involves a teacher, a structure (usually a school), and a group of students who gather together in this structure during specific times of the day to learn from the teacher. It may also include assessments and examinations carried out on paper.

Google Classroom is a platform to study online and take lessons remotely. What is it about? It is a free service of the company of Mountain View and is part of the programs present in the Google Suite. You just need an account to be able to use it. Google Classroom allows teachers to create online courses and students to participate in online lessons.

Students, for their part, can participate in real time in all courses to which they have been invited by teachers, and thus, become members of the virtual classes created by their teachers. They can also write on the course board by interacting with classmates or asking for information and advice from teachers. This book will show you how to get started with Google Classroom. Without further ado let's get started.

CHAPTER 1:

Overview of Digital Teaching

Being a teacher in the times of the internet is a challenge and a stimulus at the same time. If it is true that the use of new media includes a greater commitment, because there are new skills to learn and new tools to be able to use, it is equally true that the internet offers different possibilities to manage the class and innovative methods of organization and teaching.

As all professionals enrolled in their respective orders will know, fulfilling the obligation of continuing education is an inescapable duty, but it is not always easy to participate in conferences and classroom courses, take exams, and increase skills by acquiring professional experience. Often reaching the buildings where classes are held and moving from place to place is not compatible with the needs and schedules of professional workers.

This is why online learning is also increasingly taking ahold of the world of continuing education, with the appearance of the E-learning. Let's find out what it is.

If you want to give this term a dictionary definition, we could say that it is a form of remote learning carried out through multimedia courses, delivered through the internet on special platforms (e-learning platforms). In recent years, training projects have taken advantage of this method of learning, which goes well with the characteristics of Distance Learning.

Advantages and Disadvantages of E-learning

E-learning has therefore combined traditional lessons and new technologies, providing clear, precise, and direct training paths that fulfill the educational, training, and professionalizing functions, while taking into account the interests and needs of the user who can manage the course of the lessons in full autonomy. However, like everything else, it has pros and cons, and knowing them is the only way to make a plausible judgment on its effectiveness.

<u>Pros</u>

Let us now specifically evaluate the advantages that have made this mode of learning so famous:

☐ Possibility to view lessons multiple times if necessary; the ability to customize the structure of content and the time to dedicate to it

☐ Lower cost compared to traditional classroom training

☐ The ability to rely on software that verifies and certifies the level of learning; multimedia lessons and more interactive; using audio and animation captures the attention of the learner

☐   Standardization of the teaching method and standardization of the levels of knowledge of the participants

☐   The possibility to carry out updates quickly and promptly.

Cons

The downside of the coin is:

☐   Some people may blame the lack of direct interaction with the teacher.

☐   The absence of other students could reduce competitiveness and the motivation to learn.

As you can see, it is a social motivation rather than a didactic one. Above all, the cons are subjective disadvantages that not all individuals encounter; on the contrary, e-learning is transparent and has clear advantages.

E-learning and Professional Training

E-learning is still a real ongoing revolution, and the impact on the training system is considerable and is growing day by day. Just think of e-learning in the world of work, and the positive contribution it has made to the professional categories that need to obtain professional credits to continue training.

Many professionals have chosen to refine their skills through online training courses that can offer complete and effective teaching proposals that are in step with the times, user friendly, and, above all, certified and recognized by the membership orders.

The possibility to schedule the lessons and carry them out in the spare time has certainly been the added value par excellence, as the classic classroom courses are often held at times that do not match the work needs of professionals.

CHAPTER 2:

Introduction to Google Classroom

The Modern Teacher

One of the first questions that you may have about Google Classroom is what this platform is can do. There are quite a few different platforms that are similar to this one, so you may be curious as to how this one is going to be the best option for you compared to the other ones. You are not only going to get some of the great features that come with Google and what you are familiar with, which is one of the main benefits that you will see when working in Google Classroom.

Luckily, there are quite a few different things that you will be able to work with when working in Google Classroom. Some of the things that Google Classroom will be able to help you do include:

•Using Gmail at school. As a teacher, you will be able to create your own Gmail account. You won't have to worry about the ads or any other delays that are common with some of the other email services. Many people are familiar with Gmail, so you will be happy to use this more often.

•As a teacher, you will find that working with Google Classroom is going to help you to streamline your class. You will be able to do this by creating your assignments, being able to share your assignments and announcements with ease. You can even grade them without wasting a lot of time.

•It is easy for both the teachers and the students to work together through docs. You will be able to create as well as edit various presentations, documents, and spreadsheets inside of your browser. In addition, you can do all of this while making sure that all of the changes are saved automatically. It is also possible for more than one person to work on something at the same time without having any issues.

•Your students will be able to share their work, as well as save their work, all on the cloud. This helps save some of the hassle and the time that is expensed in sending attachments or merging together different versions.

•The Google Calendar is a great option to use with the Google Classroom. Calendars in here can be shared. This makes it easier to plan for projects. You can also integrate them together with your hangouts, contacts, email accounts, and Google Drive.

•As the teacher, you are going to find that using Google Calendars can be great. You can put up an announcement/assignment and give it a due date. Then this due date and assignment are going to show up on the class page for all of the students that are linked to this classroom. You won't have to constantly update students about when a due date is. They just need to take a look at their own Calendar to find out this information.

• If you feel that you need to set up a website that you can use for your class, Google Classroom can help out. This is something that you could do for a specific project or event. you can set it up so that the students can create some of their own websites as well.

• If it is needed, you can conduct meetings that are face-to-face with the help of video calls to your students. This can be really efficient when a student has a quick question that they would like to have answered. Some teachers have been able to use this service in order to create their own virtual field trips.

• Sometimes the chats and the emails can be all over the place and there are too many of them. The teacher can archive these emails and chats so that they can go through them at a later time if they would like. It is also really easy to organize emails and chats so it is easier for you to use.

• It is possible to use some of the different add-on apps that you need to make more happen within the class. You could use Google(+), Blogger, and Google Groups to make the class a bit more productive than you can in a traditional classroom.

These are just a few of the things that you can do when working within Google Classroom. As the teacher, you can pick out the things that you want to do inside the classroom, and each class is going to be a little bit different. It is completely fine to mix and match things together to make them personalized for the class that you are teaching.

Pills of Mindset

Google Classroom was built for both the educator and the learner. It isn't only the teachers who can do many things with Google Classroom; students can also harness the full capabilities of this application. The student's reaction to Google Classroom is whenever the teacher, who is the main Manager of the Classroom, uploads content in the Classroom. Here are some of the various things that students can do with Google Classroom.

<u>Change Ownership</u>

When you turn in an assignment, the teacher becomes the owner of your document. You are no longer the owner, and therefore you are unable to edit the text. Turned in the wrong assignment? Simply click on the **Unsubmit** button. You would need to refresh Google Classroom once you un-submit, so that you can resend a new document.

Assignment Listings

Students can find a list of all the assignments created by teachers by clicking on the **Menu** icon located at the top left-hand corner of

Google Classroom. Practically all assignments that have not been archived can be viewed in this list.

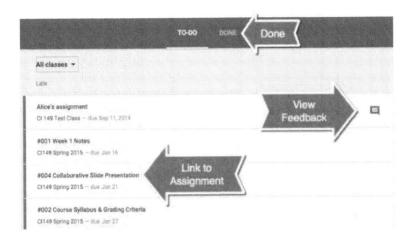

Utilize the Mobile App for Easier Access

We know students are always on their mobile phones. One of the best ways to get notified if you have a new assignment is through the Google Classroom's mobile app. The mobile app can be downloaded and installed from PlayStore or iTunes. The app allows students to view their assignments and submit their work directly from the app. This mainly works when students are requested to submit real-life samples, or a video or a combination of photos. All they need to do is take pictures of their samples or their solutions, and then upload them to the Google Classroom.

No worries if you haven't clicked on **Save**.

Encourage your students to use Google Docs to do their assignments. If you have given work that requires them to write reports, write a story, or anything that requires their use of a Word document, use Google Docs because it saves edits automatically. This eliminates your student's excuses for not being able to complete their homework because they did not save it. Also, it just makes things easier when you are so engrossed with completing your work and you forget to save; Google Docs does it for you.

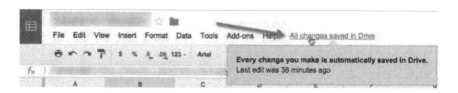

Sharing Isn't The Same Thing As Turning In

When a student clicks **Open An Assignment** to hand in their assignment, they need to click on **TURN IN**. Sharing an assignment to the Google Classroom is not the same thing as turning in your completed work. Make sure you click on TURN IN to submit your assignment in due time.

You Will Not Lose Assignments

You will not lose assignments unless you delete them. Any documents you upload to your Google Classroom are only seen by you and the teacher. Any assignments you upload to your Google Drive will be seen on the teacher's Google Drive as well. Your

Google Drive is the storage system for Google Classroom, and it works the same way for both the teacher as well as the students.

Due Dates

You'd have a harder time explaining to your teacher why you have not submitted your assignment, especially since the due dates are continuously shown on an assignment. Assignments that are not due yet are indicated on the class title on the homepage. Also, on the left side of the page, late assignments have a particular folder, where the teacher can accurately see the assignments listing from the menu icon on the upper-left corner of the page.

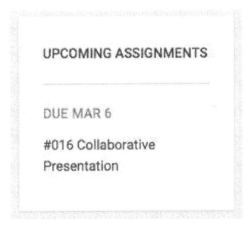

Returning an Assignment

Students working on a Google Document can return at any time to the file that they are working on. Get back to the assignment stream and click on **Open**. It will take you to a link to the documents that you have on Google Drive. Click on the document and get back right into it. You can also access this file directly from your personal Google Drive. It is the same way you click on any document on your desktop to work on it again.

The plus side is Google Docs autosaves your work.

Communicating With Teachers

It's either you communicate publicly on Google Classrooms for the entire class to see, or you communicate privately.

Communicating privately helps a lot especially for students who are shy and prefer to speak to the teacher directly without the involvement of other classmates.

It also helps the teacher speak privately to address a student's issue on an assignment without making them feel inadequate or that they have not done well.

Commenting on Assignments

Comments on an assignment are viewable by your classmates on Google Classroom when it is made on any assignments uploaded to the app.

Students just need to click on **Add Comments** under an assignment.

If students would like to communicate in private, with you, they can leave it on the assignment submission page. Within a specific document, you can use the **File** menu and click on **Email collaborators** to message or link a document to the teacher.

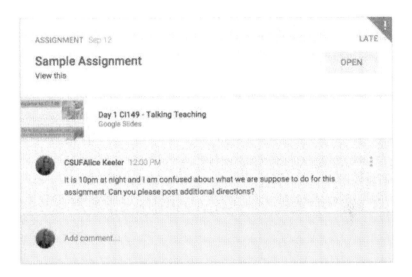

Add Additional Files To An Assignment

Students and teachers can both add additional files to an assignment. For students, they can add in files that did not come together with a template the teacher gave. You can click on **Add Additional Files** on the assignment submission page again. Links from websites can also be added. Additional files help in the attempt to provide a wholesome blended learning approach in schools, because you can add files of different formats and types.

CHAPTER 3:

Step-by-Step System to Use Google Classroom

How to Create a Class and Organize It

Creating a Class

If you are a teacher, the first thing to do after signing into your Google Classroom account is to create a class. It is within the class that you work for students and pass announcements to them.

This can be done by the steps, given below.

On the home page of your Google Classroom account, click the (+) icon to create or join a class. Choose **Create Class**.

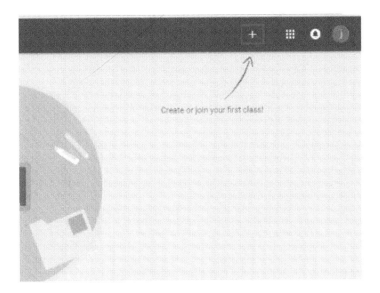

A window will pop up, asking you to confirm that you agree to the terms and conditions. Click the checkbox to activate it, and click **Continue**.

You will be taken to another window, where you will have to enter the class details. The class name is mandatory; the rest of the details are optional. Enter the class name.

In the **Section** field, you can enter a short description of the class, the grade level, and the class time.

To enter the subject for the class, click inside the **Subject** field, and enter it there. You can also select from the options provided as you type. This field is also optional.

Create class

Class name (required)
Class 1

Section
Computer Science Monday 8-11 AM

Subject
Automata Theory

Room
RCL Room 1

CANCEL   CREATE

The location of the class can be entered into the **Room** field. Just click inside the field, and enter the place where you will be holding the class.

Once you have filled all the details, click the **CREATE** button to create the class.

All new classes come with a **Classwork** page, but you are allowed to remove this. Even after removing it, the class teacher is allowed to add it back.

Setting Up the Classroom

Setting up your classroom is easier than you think. While a lot of other learning platforms ask you to jump through hoops and learn a lot of different tabs before getting to use the system, Google Classroom tries to keep it simple. Some of the things that you need to do to start with Classroom are explained next.

Visit *classroom.google.com*. You will be able to sign up for an account using your school email address. If your school administrator has some special rules about which emails to use, you will need to talk to them.

Click the **(+)** that is located on the right on top of the page. This allows you to create the first class. Click **Create Class**.

Name the class so that it is easy to remember. Consider not only the name of the class but also the section. This is important if you are teaching more than one section of the same class. You can name it something like 'Senior English: Period 2.' Name the class as you want; just think about how you will recognize it later.

Now that the class is created, your students can join it. You can send the link to the students in your class to ensure they get into the right section. While waiting for students to join, be a bit creative. Change the theme to either make it match the course name or just do something you like.

Do not forget to fill the **About** section.

This is going to be useful to students before starting your class because it gives them some information about the course.

Place information, such as your email, the syllabus, grading scale, and other information, that the students may need throughout the year.

Daily Use of Classroom

Once your Classroom is set up and students start to join, it is up to you to have fun with the layout and make the platform work for you.

There are some things that you can do with this platform to help students learn, including the below.

Make Announcements: This helps you communicate with the whole class. Simply click on the **Announcement** button, and write the message you want. It is possible to attach links, YouTube videos, and files from your Google Drive to the announcement if needed.

Follow the same procedure used for announcements; thus, you can create a new assignment. Simply write the name of the assignment, a short description, and attach any files that are necessary. Make sure to add the due date so students can prepare.

Manage Students: To manage your students, go to the **Students** tab. From here, you can allow students to comment, post, or just read the material.

You can send emails to one or two students at a time, and even remove them from the class if they end up switching.

Grading Assignments: After the assignment deadline is up, you can click on a student's name to see the files attached.

You can then click on **No Grade**, and then place the grade that you want to give them. If the system automatically graded a student based on your settings, you can always go back in and change the grade. Make sure to hit **Return** when done, to save the changes.

How to Manage a Class

The first thing that you can do when changing the class and managing it, is to give it a theme.

One thing you will notice is that you do not have students in there as soon as it is created, so you can have a bit of fun with it. One way to do this is, on the right side near the header of the general class, you can change the class theme.

You can use the themes that are provided. Some photos of classes themselves are good options

You can use different templates for each one so that you know exactly what theme you are using, because they can sometimes be a bit complicated.

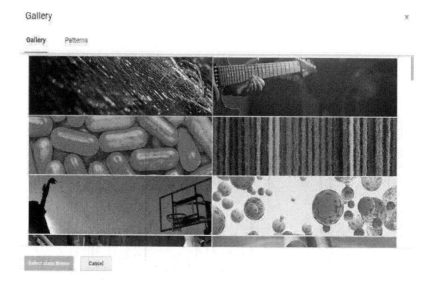

How to Remove, Delete and View a Class

When using Google Classroom, sometimes you may want to delete a class when it is the end of the semester. You can always restore it again if you need to, as well. You can also delete it if you either never want to see that class again, or you have no use for it because you have the assignments already. Now, if you do not archive these, they will stick around, so make sure that you archive them first.

Archived classes essentially mean that they are in an area where you have the same materials the work students have, and the posts. You can view them, but you cannot actually use them. This is good if a student wants the materials.

Archiving classes is simple to do. You choose the class, press the three-dotted button, and presto! It is archived.

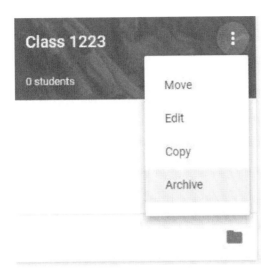

Now to view an archived class after it is been archived, you press the **More** menu (three-lined button) again. Go down to the tab that says **Archive**, and then choose the class you want to see.

To delete a class though, you need to do the same thing. Remember, that you need to archive the class before you can delete it, so scroll all the way down and choose **Archive**. Once you have the classes, you need to press **More** (three-dotted button) and then choose **Delete**. From there, you will have the class fully removed. Remember though, you cannot undo this once you have done it. If you do choose to delete a class, you do not have access to the comments or the posts; but if you have any files that are in the Drive, you can always access those, since you have those in the class files themselves.

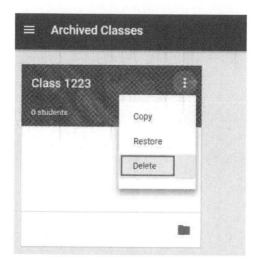

There are a few class management things that you can implement, and some tips and tricks of Google Classroom. The first thing that happens, is that when you get to the **Classes** tab, you can drag and move the classes around. This is a good way to change the order of things, and it is quite easy to do. Another important thing to remember is that you have the **Classroom** function. It is quite handy, and if you want to change the calendar or view it, you can essentially press the icon with the calendar. You can even check it out to see what is coming up for every single class, because some classes may do certain things at different times of the semester.

Finally, you can always adjust the settings at any point. This is done with the buttons that you see on the home screen. Here, you can change the name of the class, especially if it is confusing; show the class code if you need it; and also decide on the Stream, and show whether or not you want items to be deleted or displayed. There are other features there too. They are all right there, waiting to be used.

When it comes to Google Classroom, knowing how to create the classes is a big part of it. If you have classes that you want to add, or you want to get started with Google Classroom, this is the way to go, and it is the surefire way to success.

Ms. Smith's Math Class

General

Class code

Stream

Show deleted items
Only teachers can view deleted items.

How You Can Manage the Due Dates, Homework, And Assignments

Using Google Docs with Assignments

In making an assignment, there will be times when you want to add a document to Google Docs. Those can be helpful when offering long directions, research guides, and other content.

When you add these types of files, you will want to make sure that you select the appropriate setting for how your students will access it. After adding one to the task, you can find a drop-down menu of three choices.

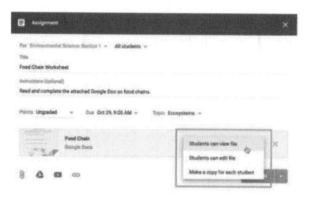

Let us take a look at how you may want to use each of these options:

Students can access the file: Use this option if the file is just something you want your students to access, but do not want them to make any changes to.

Students can edit the file: This choice can be beneficial if you have a document that you want your students to work with or to fill out together.

Make a copy for each student: If you have a workbook or document that you want each student to complete individually, this choice would create a different copy of the same document for each student.

Using Topics

On the **Classwork** page, you can use themes to organize and group your assignments and resources. To create a subject, click the **Create** button, and then pick **Subject**.

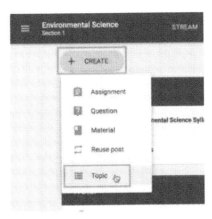

Topics will help you coordinate your content around the different units you teach during the year. You may also use it to divide your content by form, break it into assignments, classwork, readings, and other subject areas.

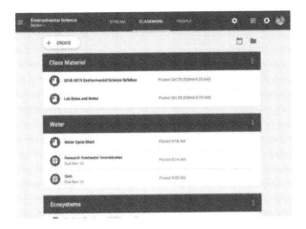

Create Group Documents

The first thing is to create a document for the assignment. They can include sheets, documents, etc. Duplicate every group. Ensure that you add the name of the group, or include a number at the end of the file name for easy identification and assistance. Users can store group assignments inside the Drive, so they can locate the stored document easily. It is also very easy to store documents in the folder of the classroom.

Create A Topic for Group Assignment

Proceed to the tab **Class**; click on the **Create** button and select the topic. Find a suitable name for the project, input it, and then save it.

Select Students

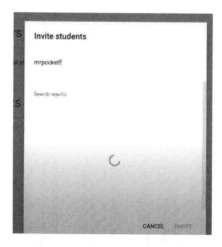

The first thing to do is to tap on the **Create** control key and select **Assignment**. When you get to the dialogue box of **Assignment**, select the drop-down menu for **Students**, and unmark every student.

Then, select the number of students that you want inside the group. If you want to create another group or more, you should repeat the same.

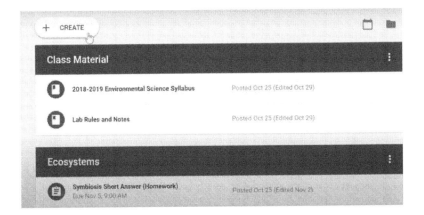

Create Homework

Proceed to the dialogue box of **Homework,** and find a suitable title for the homework or project; include the name of the group or additional instructions. Now click on the **Group Task** topic; now you can give the group a task to perform. Now assign the task, and ensure that you select students who can edit in the options, instead of creating another copy for every student. Users should create a draft for the task before they create the group.

Reuse One Assignment for More Groups

One exciting feature of the Classroom is the **Reuse** attribute, which helps teachers a lot. It helps them avoid typing information all over again for each student inside the group. The first thing to do is to select the **Create** control key, and tap **Reuse Post**; the dialogue box for the reuse post will display. Click on the post that you want to duplicate, and tap **Reuse**. Now you can edit the project you want for the groups. Make sure that you adjust the group members through the drop-down of the **Student** menu, and ensure that you change the number of the group within the controls and title, if necessary. Also, you should not forget to remove the homework for a particular group when you want to create a new group. If you do not want to post the homework at the time of creating the group, you can save it inside the draft folder, and utilize it at a later date.

Post Group Assignments

Whenever you complete the draft of the group assignment, the last step is posting it inside the group, so that the students can have access to the project, and can start working. You will find the draft containing the homework that you create beneath the group topic that you create. Select **More** (three-dotted button), and tap **Edit**. The conversation box of the homework will show according to what you post. You can perform the same task whenever you want to post it to the groups.

CHAPTER 4:

Tips and Tricks

1. Create each teacher with class details and data.

2. Time planning and inventory formation.

Each teacher spends a day with continuous professional development in various tasks and therefore receives the included assistance for all teachers, who seek clear help in putting their lessons together.

3. Check your server.

Everything you do from a school server may require more restrictions than usual. Be sure to check with your IT specialist that what you're planning isn't too out of the box.

4. Don't be too careful.

Jennie Devine, Director of the Louis International School in Milan, which closed for more than three weeks, praised less while teaching remotely. *"In the beginning, we tried to make videos, worksheets, quizzes, and so on.*

The students said the results were confusing and they didn't know in what order they had to work," he explained. *"We are now working to focus on the training video (perhaps in two parts) and some quick tests or other training material. "*

5. Make a daily schedule.

Odell and Devine agree that a plan is necessary and must be followed. Odell recommends organizing data for the classes every day. You start each exercise with Google Hangouts in the classroom. Then, students can ask questions in the classroom.

Students can finish their work and put it in the classroom.

"We can do it without a long journey, without completing their work on this path," said Odell. Devine suggests that fair guidelines help keep the strategic distance from the recurring ad blocking problems.

"You have to define certain standards and practices. Opinions should not surround the work and use previous comments before presenting the research," he said.

6. Check your settings.

If you are not careful, you can cancel the notification: change the settings so as not to include ads when someone comments on a document. You have to be able to turn it off when you go - follow your work schedule and don't let your computer ruin your life.

7. Be realistic and clear in your instructions.

Devine said that not all students have a home printer, so make sure every activity is possible without printing extra items.

"I feel that the company is very transparent," said Odell. *"If students believe that their technical skills cannot edit/edit documents, they will use the Google Docs connecting link. I can send feedback directly from their documents. "*

If you don't think it will work for you, prepare another class assignment to secure work, another framework you should try. *"I've discovered that a daily program called* Attach Jobs Here *works well for my students,"* Devine said. *"Students can do all the homework at the same time and see who does the work. Otherwise, students will start working with the video exercise, and it can be very confusing if there is more than one video."*

8. There are no faces in the video.

"All students need to know that they should shut down their cameras while using Google Hangout with teachers," Odell said. This should be done from the beginning and all students should know that they do not show their faces when talking to the teacher.

9. Share your logo.

Security rules require staff members and IT pioneers to share teacher access and not talk about teachers intimately. Employers must constantly monitor the content of messages.

The teacher should talk to the students about what the school allows and also inform the students the mode of communication to expect from the teacher, and inform all other correspondences.

10. Talk to caregivers and parents.

Use classrooms to care for caregivers and parents. You can invite caregivers and parents to email daily or weekly summaries of what is happening in their children's lessons. The message includes the work of missing or incoming students, as well as questions and requests that they posted in class.

11. Help students organize their own Google Calendar.

As a result, Google Classes creates a calendar for each class and updates the calendar with future work hours and students. Students can also monitor events such as field trips and study days. The calendar makes tracking easy. As new projects or deadlines change; students will always see the latest information.

12. Promote collaboration.

The teacher can assign assignments and send notifications to select students or groups of students in the classroom. This tool allows teachers to identify strategies from variables as well as assist in collaborative teamwork.

13. Use comments for the versatile app in the classroom.

Teachers and students can use the Class app on iOS, Android, and Chrome phones. You can provide ongoing feedback by reporting on student work in this program. Likewise, students can comment on their homework to better express concepts or ideas.

14. Discover the combination of a Class with other devices.

Google Classroom uses an API to control the interface and exchange information with many of your favorite devices. There are a number of scripts and web pages to deal with, including Active Learning, Pear Deck, Newels, and many more.

15. Encourage administrators to use Google Classrooms.

While this aspect is for leaders and not for teachers, it is still important here. Administrators can see information such as the number of classes, the number of assignments, and which teacher uses the tools to manage learning. Access to this data can help teachers.

Google Classroom Can Help with Home-Schooling

Are you a teacher or a student in a course? A free Google Classroom service can also support both students and teachers. This is the beginning of education and care in a school that has different characteristics.

The difficulty in learning is communication. This is regularly monitored by the educational platform purchased by the school for others. Google Classroom can be an interesting and free solution.

This service was originally integrated into the education system but has been available to everyone since 2017. The main requirement is that everyone who uses it must have a free Google account and, of course, a PC or Chromebook. To access everything in one place, setting up Google Classroom is easy. As a teacher, you can create pages for each group or class and then invite students. You can send messages to all selected students or students through Google Classroom and you can schedule this communication.

The most important role is to create learning content. To do this, you can use tools such as documents, spreadsheets, and presentations, and also have a shared folder on Google drive so you can share a lot of data. To make sure students have learned something, you can ask questions. Make learning more fun when you collect everything in Google's classrooms. As a teacher, you can easily track student activities and make comments. However, with Google's ongoing service, we must not forget that everything we do here is used by organizations to collect customer data.

Functions and Categories of Google

1. Menu

Lists, calendars, class lists, and much more can be done here.

2. Stream

Post classwork, ask questions, and create content and assignments in the classroom. Google Classroom helps you organize and mark your activities.

3. People

All student data is collected here - and a student can be excluded from the course.

4. Settings

Change your settings to find other routes to other Google services.

5. Class Code

This code allows students to become members of the course. Here you can change the image of the theme.

6. Comments

Share activities, files, and class links.

7. Message

Send a message to the class; everyone can comment.

CHAPTER 5:

Tools and Extensions

Many education apps work with Google Classroom.

U se this listing to investigate apps you are currently using, or find new ones that will permit you to share effectively with Google Classroom.

Did you understand that Google Classroom integrates well with others?

It's hard to believe, but it's true! Google is known for making their apps open to working with outside apps, and Google Classroom is no different.

I have assembled a list of several apps that incorporate with Google Classroom, making it much simpler to create messages and lessons with your favorite resources and apps.

How to Use These Apps with Google Classroom?

The vast majority of the apps below function with Google Classroom through a **Share** button. This association permits you to use a portion of your preferred sites and apps routinely with Google Classroom.

Note: Some of these apps are free, but not all.

To use the app with Google Classroom:

1. Create an account on the website or app.

2. Create or locate the resources or activity within a website or app.

3. Use the **Share to Classroom** option within the chosen app. (The first time you use the association you should allow authorizations to access your account.)

4. This association or connection will permit you to do things like making a test and send it to one of your classes in Google Classroom.

Actively Learn

Actively Learn works flawlessly with Google Classroom. Teachers can, without much difficulty, synchronize Classroom programs to Actively Learn and adjust Actively Learn grades and assignments back to Google Classroom.

Additio App

Additio App is a suite for teachers to remain in control and easily contact students and families. It offers numerous helpful tools, similar to an amazing grade book and a strong exercise organizer.

Aeries

Teachers can connect to or make new Classroom classes dependent on their Aeries classes, and import scores into the Aeries grade book.

Aladdin

With this connected to Classroom, classes can be integrated with classes in Aladdin. Grades and assignments can also be matched up among Aladdin and Classroom.

Alma

Alma is the principal Student Information System to incorporate directly with Google Classroom. With this connected, teachers can synchronize grades and assignments, and tech groups can manage Google Classroom classes over their schools and locale.

American Museum of Natural History

Educational K-12 projects and resources from the American Museum of Natural History are available. Use the **Share to Classroom** button to share applicable articles, resources, and curriculum.

Aristotle Insight: K12

Enable students to become insightful, with this all-in-one borderless classroom management.

BookWidgets

BookWidgets gives layouts for interactive activities. Teachers can pick between more than 40 distinct gadgets or layouts to connect with students.

BrainPOP

With BrainPOP, teachers can import their classes legitimately from Google Classroom into My BrainPOP. SSO-prepared student accounts are made when a teacher imports a class, permitting students to sign in to BrainPOP through the Google launcher menu.

Buncee

A creation and introduction apparatus for students and teachers to make interactive classroom content permits students of any age to visualize concepts and communicate creatively. Just build a task, note, class update, action, or undertaking, and share it with the students in your Google Classroom.

CK-12

The CK-12 Foundation gives a library of free online videos, textbooks, flashcards, exercises, and genuine apps for more than 5,000 subjects, from Arithmetic to History.

CodeHS

CodeHS is a far-reaching platform for helping schools teach software engineering.

They offer online educational plans, teaching aids and resources, and professional advancement.

Curiosity.com

Their point of interest is to ignite curiosity and inspire individuals to learn. Every day, they make and publish engaging topics for many interested students around the world.

Desmos

An assortment of remarkable and engaging digital math activities, which are free for you and your students.

Discovery Education

Discovery Education ignites student interest and moves instructors to rethink learning, with award-winning advanced content and professional improvement.

Dogo News

DOGO Media is the main online network enabling children to see news using online media in a fun, protected, and social environment.

Used by a large number of students and teachers from around the globe, their sites have immediately become a network of children and instructors connecting with recent developments, books, and films.

DuoLingo

Numerous teachers and even entire governments around the globe now see Duolingo as the ideal blended learning ally for their language classrooms. Duolingo exercises give every student personalized practice and feedback, enabling them to take advantage of classroom guidance.

Edcite

Teachers can import their class programs from Google Classroom into Edcite, and afterward, send Edcite assignments to their students in the classroom. When students get to these assignments, they are automatically signed into their Edcite accounts using a single sign-on method.

EdPuzzle

Create an interactive video lesson, include your magical touch, and track your student's understanding. With the EDpuzzle integration, teachers can import all Classroom courses and students at sign up.

Edulastic

Synchronizing with Google Classroom makes class lists in Edulastic and stays up-to-date. Teachers would then be able to share Edulastic appraisals directly in student's classroom feeds, thereby permitting them to get to the task without entering another password or going to the Edulastic site.

Engage NY

With EngageNY in the classroom, students get immediate feedback on their work, with repeat attempts if necessary, while teachers can without much difficulty access information to drive their in-class instruction.

Explain Everything

Thanks to this Google Classroom incorporation, teachers and administrators can flawlessly oversee licenses using Explain Everything Discover.

Flat

Teachers can make music composition and structure assignments in Google Classroom using Flat Education, online music documentation programming. Teachers can synchronize existing Classroom lists and structure new music exercises that are open to students from the classroom.

Flipgrid

Flipgrid is a site that permits teachers to make 'frameworks' of short conversation style questions that students react to through recorded videos. Every framework is a message board where teachers can pose questions, and their students can post 90-second video reactions that show up in a tiled "grid" show. Effectively share links to Flipgrids and add them to assignments in Google Classroom.

Familiarity Tutor for Google

Familiarity Tutor is an online app that has tools to allow students to work on reading out loud and to record sections, called appraisals or tests. Effectively you can assign reading sections as assignments in Google Classroom.

Gale Cengage Learning

Gale examination resources incorporate novel online databases, essential library sources, advanced paper files, courses, eBooks, and print books.

GAT+

Monitor student's conduct on Chrome devices and G Suites with this audit and security apparatus.

GeoGebra

GeoGebra's K-12+ STEM educational program materials can be embedded into Google Classroom as activities with only a couple of clicks. More than 700,000 materials (in addition to more included every day!) are accessible to meet the STEM needs of teachers and students.

GoGuardian

GoGuardian Teacher permits teachers to allow indication of the classrooms they've set up in the Classroom, and adjusting student enlistment, class period, and subject across platforms. Teachers and students can profit considerably more from their Chromebooks with streamlined usage and setup.

Google Cast for Education

Google Cast for Education is a free Chrome app that permits students and teachers to share their screens remotely from anyplace in the classroom.

The cast for education has built-in controls for teachers and permits them to easily add students from the classroom.

InsertLearning

InsertLearning is a Chrome augmentation that lets you transform sites into intelligent exercises.

You can include notes, videos, discussion questions, links, multiple-choice questions, and more! Then, effectively share your exercise with students in Google Classroom.

Kami

With the Kami app, teachers can transform assignments, worksheets, and educational program resources in PDF format, for students to finish and then submit.

Kodable

Kodable instructs children to code at home or school with fun games. It gives teachers a total K-5 coding educational plan for the classroom.

LearnZillion

LearnZillion is a site that furnishes teachers with a library of intelligent math and language art exercises, quizzes, videos, and assignments for students.

Little SIS for Classroom

Little SIS for Classroom creates Google Classroom classes and auto-synchronizes class lists from student data, making it simpler for schools to embrace and keep up with Google Classroom.

Listenwise

Listenwise is an award-winning listening ability platform. They harness the intensity of tuning in to propel education and learning in all students.

Their assortment of digital recordings and open radio continues instruction associated with current reality, and builds student listening aptitudes simultaneously.

LucidPress

Lucidpress is an online drag-and-drop publishing app, enabling anybody to make stunning material for digital and print.

Makers Empire 3D

Makers Empire 3D is intended to help K-8 teachers coordinate 3D plans and printing into their teaching practice efficiently and effectively.

Math Games

This integration aligns Classroom with *MathGames.com*, a hotspot for math games and aptitude practice on the web.

Teachers can automatically create and match up math assignments within the classroom and keep tabs on a student's development.

Nearpod

Nearpod is a student engagement platform that can be used to amazing extent in Classroom. The app's idea is basic: a teacher can make presentations that can contain quizzes, videos, polls, images, web content, drawing-boards, etc.

NetTrekker

It permits teachers and students to look through 360,000+ educator-vetted guidelines and adjusted open-education resources, all in one place.

OpenEd.com

Teachers can assign OpenEd assessments, games, videos, and repeat questions with a single click, and finished assignments will be stamped "Done." OpenEd additionally gives group and single sign-on, so all classes and students will be matched up routinely.

CHAPTER 6:

Google Classroom Student's View

Create An Account and Log In

Go to *https://classroom.google.com/* and click on the **Sign in** button.

S tudents can either use their Gmail IDs or the school login credentials for this account.

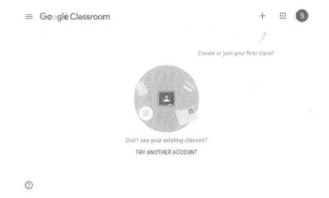

After being logged in, students will be displayed in already enrolled classes. If this is the first time for students to use the Google Classroom, they have to enroll in the new class by clicking on the (+) button at the top-right corner of the screen and click **Join Class**. (e.g., the student already had the class joining code (i.e. gqjczi4) so by simply entering the code, they are enrolled in this class).

Class code
Ask your teacher for the class code, then enter it here.

Class code

gqjczi4

To sign in with a class code
- Use an authorized account
- Use a class code with 5-7 letters or numbers, and no spaces or symbols

If you have trouble joining the class, go to the Help Center article

Now, the students can either join the class by accepting the invitation email from the teacher or simply go to **Join Class** and enter the code provided by the teacher.

Note: This needs to be only done once. After they have enrolled in the class, they'll remain a member of the Classroom for the remaining academic semester/year.

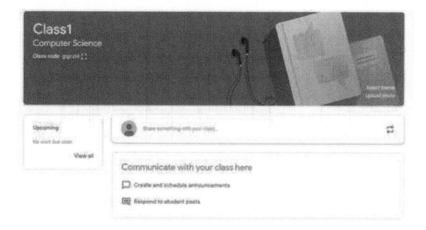

Viewing and Accessing Homework

To check homework or tasks set, after signing in, the students have to click on the class they want to check. For instance, in this class, a teacher named Barira has assigned a task to her English class, to write a summary of *How to Kill a Mockingbird.*

Once the students have clicked on the desired class, the student will be in the Google Classroom. They'll be able to see three tabs on the top: **Stream**, **People**, and **Classwork**.

The Stream Page

•The Stream looks almost like a social networking page. The latest post by the teacher, added in Google Classroom, will be visible at the top, and the oldest post will be available at the bottom. Each post will be related to the subject that the students are learning with this teacher. For instance, here, Miss Barira has given an assignment titled "Write a summary of *How to Kill a Mockingbird.*" The description elaborates to write a single page summary of the novel, including the details and vocabulary you have learned in the lesson. It is a marked assignment for 100 points.

• The student will be able to access the task assigned by the teacher, and it will contain the title, description of the assignment, and the instructions regarding the assignment. It will also have a submission deadline, including the date and time.

• The task can be graded or ungraded as well, depending on the teacher's will.

• The teacher also guides students on whether the task has to be completed offline or online.

Completing/Submitting the Assignment Online

If the students are asked to complete the assignment online, they will have to open the assignment and then click on the **Add or create** (+) tab followed by a drop-down menu. From here, the students can choose to create a Google document or upload a file from their devices or online Google Drive.

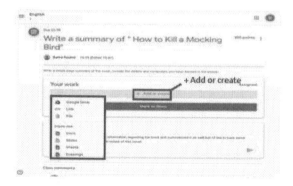

When they choose the document, it will be previewed in the white box just above the **Add or create** (+) button. (e.g., in this case, the student has browsed their device and uploaded a .docx file as their complete assignment)

OR

If the student has to create a new document, they'll go to the **Create new section,** click on the document, and start working on it. The file will open in a new tab and can be saved automatically until closed. The students can access this document to work on it as many times as they want to until they have to submit it.

●File attachments. Attach files, import files from Google Drive, use YouTube videos, or add links of websites.

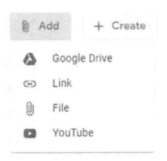

Insert files from Google Drive.

Add a link.

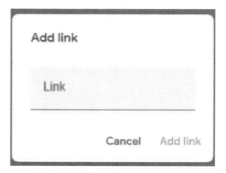

Add a file from the device.

After completion and when the assignment has been added, the student needs to use the **Hand in** button.

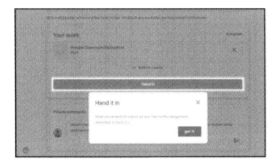

Completing Work Offline

If the students are asked to complete the assignment offline, they'll only have to access the instructions from Google Classroom. When they have completed the assignment, they'll open the assignment and simply click on the **Mark as Done** button. This will notify the teacher the students have completed their work on time for the submission deadline.

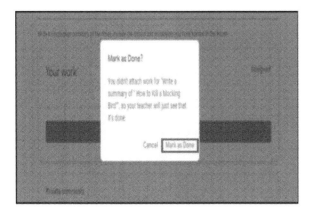

The People Page

The students can view the teachers/co-teacher and other students of this class on the **People** Page. For instance, in this case, there is only a single teacher, Barira Rashid.

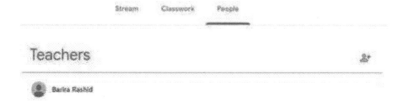

The Classwork Page

On this page, the students can view other useful links, documents, and websites associated with the course/subject they are taking.

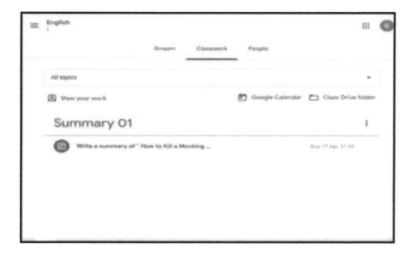

CHAPTER 7:

Learn More About
The Google Classroom Platform

Google Classroom News

What's New in the Google Classroom

The drag-and-drop on the Classwork page.

This is a sort of new Classwork page where educators can remain made with chart their classes. In any case, we comprehend that teachers sort out their classes explicitly propensities and need extra adaptability in their classroom tools. So now, you can relocate whole topics and individual Classwork items, altering them effectively on the page. You can drag a whole point to a particular zone on the Classwork page, or drag singular things inside—and in—topics. This accommodation pushed a year earlier on versatility, and now it's the ideal, open entryway for it to hit the web.

The Invigorated Us

Directly from now, you'll persistently observe that Classroom has a superior look and sentiments, first on the page, and soon in the Classroom versatile applications. Over the last couple of years, we recognizable Google's new material subject as having more consistency across Google products and platforms. Among the changes, you'll see an unyieldingly normal game plan stream— despite another way to deal with overseeing shape, covering, iconography, and typography, on both the web and the advantageous application.

We're besides making the class code less hard to access and experience, so students can without a truly amazing stretch find and join.

At long last, we're giving 78 new topics custom portrayals, ranging from History to Math to Hairdressing to Photography. Eventually, you can re-attempt your Classroom like never before as of now.

Refreshed Training and Backing

At last, with its new tools and progressively, different changes come essentially for much better help.

In the Teacher Social order, you'll find resuscitated records in our First Day of Classroom training with the new course of action and highlights we turned out in 2018.

While we're pounding perpetually, we assembled a predominant than whenever in late memory Help Center, got along with our District and thing gathering.

The Following Are Past Changes To Google Classroom:

Other/Past Changes to Google Classroom Before the 2019-2020 School Year

Post Questions

Phan clarifies, *"You can present inquiries on your group and permit students to have conversations by reacting to one another's answers (or not, contingent upon the setting you pick.)*

For instance, you could post a video and ask students to answer an inquiry about it, or post an article and request that they compose a passage accordingly."

Reuse Assignments

If you reuse educational programs quite a long time after year, or if nothing else, reuse archives, there is an update you may like.

Phan clarifies, *"Presently you can reuse assignments, declarations or inquiries from any of your classes — or any class you co-educate, regardless of whether it's from a year ago or a week ago.*

When you pick what you'd prefer to duplicate, you'll have the option to make changes before you post or dole out it."

Improved Calendar Reconciliation

We love changes that improve the work procedure. In the next month, Classroom will, therefore, make a calendar for all of your classes in Google Calendar. All assignments with a due date will be normally added to your gathering calendar and kept awake with the most recent. You'll have the choice to see your calendar from inside Classroom or on Google Calendar, where you can truly incorporate class events, like field trips or guest speaker sessions.

Knock a Post

Staying posts on sites, tweets, or Facebook refreshes has, for quite some time, been a thing. Presently you can do it on Google Classroom, too, by moving any post to the top.

Due Dates Discretionary

Undertaking based learning, self-coordinated learning? Creator Ed? If you utilize long-haul ventures or other assignments without due dates, you would now be able to make assignments without due dates in Google Classroom.

Connect a Google Form to a Post

In case you're an aficionado of Google Forms (here's a post about utilizing Google Forms to make a self-evaluated test), this is a chance you'll appreciate. Phan clarifies, *"Numerous teachers have been utilizing Google Forms as a simple method to relegate a test or study to the class. Coming in the following weeks, teachers and students will before long have the option to append Google Forms from Drive to posts and assignments, and get a connection in Classroom to see the appropriate responses handily."*

YouTube Usefulness

Do you love YouTube, yet get stressed over stunning content? Google hears you. Since it in like manner contains content that an organization or school presumably won't consider commendable, a month prior, we moved advanced YouTube settings for all Google Applications spaces as an Additional Help. These settings empower Applications overseers to keep the YouTube chronicles detectable for set apart in users, similarly, as set apart out users on frameworks supervised by the manager.

Ways to Utilize Google Classroom

When a task, exercise, or unit doesn't work, include your remarks or have students include their input. Label it or save it to an alternate folder for correction.

•Adjust the educational program to different teachers.

•Offer information with a professional learning network.

•Keep tests of model composition for arranging.

•Label your educational program.

•Request day-by-day, week-after-week, by-semester, or annual criticism from students and guardians utilizing Google Forms.

•Offer unknown composing tests to students.

•See what your assignments resemble from the students' perspective.

•Flip your classroom. The tools to distribute recordings and offer assignments are centered on Google Applications for Training.

•Impart task standards with students.

•Let students pose inquiries secretly.

•Let students make their computerized arrangement of their preferred work.

•Make a rundown of endorsed inquiries about sources. You can likewise separate this by student, gathering, understanding level. That's just the beginning.

•Post a declaration for students, or students and guardians.

•Plan progressively versatile learning encounters for your students– in higher education, for instance.

•Have students outline their development after some time utilizing Google Sheets.

•Offer due dates with coaches outside the classroom with an open calendar.

•E-mail students separately or in groups. Even better, watch as they speak with each other.

•Make tests that grade themself utilizing Google Forms.

•Control file rights (see, alter, duplicate, download) on a file-by-file premise.

•Have student's clergyman, venture-based, learning antiquities.

•As a teacher, you can work together with different teachers (same evaluation by group, same content across the grade level.)

•Support advanced citizenship using a shared connection that is recorded.

•Use Google Calendar for due dates, occasions outside the classroom, and other significant 'sequential information.'

•Discuss carefully with students who might be reluctant to 'talk' with you face-to-face.

•Smooth out cross-curricular tasks with different teachers.

•Total and distribute normally got to sites to ensure everybody has the same access, same archives, same connections, and same information.

•Vertically-adjusted students are learning by creating and sharing "milestone" student assignments that reflect the dominance of explicit measures.

•Empower a typical language by unloading principles and offer area-wide.

•Urge students to utilize their cell phones for formal learning. By getting to archives, YouTube channels, group correspondence, advanced portfolio pieces, and more on a BYOD gadget, students will get an opportunity to consider them to be different options from an only for-diversion gadget.

•Make and distribute 'power gauges' (with students, different teachers, and different schools) for straightforwardness and coordinated effort.

•Elevate distributed as well as school-to-class communications students with different students, students with different teachers, and teachers with different teachers.

•Make 'by-need' groups as classes–dependent on understanding level, for instance.

•Check which students have gotten to which assignments.

•Give the students input.

•Add voice remarks to student composing (this requires an outsider application to do).

•Assist students with making content-heavy YouTube channels.

•'Shut circuit distribute' commented on exploring papers as indicated by explicit styles (MLA, APA, and so on) or other something else 'confounding' work.

•Make an advanced parking garage for questions.

•Control computerized leave slips.

•Rather than schoolwork, give out willful 'exercise extensions' for students. When questions emerge about authority or evaluations, allude to who got to and finished what and when.

•Make folders of incidental exercise materials—advanced adaptations of writings, and so forth.

•Appreciate more brilliant conferencing with students and guardians with simple to-get-to-work, information, composing, input, get to information, etc.

•Save PDFs or different depictions of advanced assets, in general, got to folders.

•Make an information divider, however, with spreadsheets and shading coding.

•Make sub-work or make-up work simple to get to.

•Gather information. This can occur in an assortment of ways, from utilizing Google Forms, extraction to Google Sheets, or your in-house strategy.

•Give briefs; they are critical for learning.

•See who finished what–and when initially.

•Track when students turn-in work.

•Since getting to be followed, search for designs in student propensities those that get to assignments quickly, those that reliably come back to work, etc. Share those patterns (namelessly) with students as a method of conveying "best practices in learning" for students who may not think of them.

•Particularly guidance, through tiering, gathering, or Sprout's spiraling.

•Make groups that are dependent on preparation, enthusiasm, understanding level, or different variables for instructing and learning.

•Use Google Forms to survey students and make per user intrigue reviews. And that's only the tip of the iceberg.

•Model a work referred to the page.

•Make reference sheets.

•Structure computerized group building exercises.

•Make a paperless classroom.

•Offer all-inclusive and as often as possible got to assignments–ventures rules, year-long due dates, math formulas, content-regional realities, recorded courses of events, and so forth.

CHAPTER 8:

How to Motivate Students to Use Google Classroom?

Motivation is, in reality, one of the critical pillars of a successful classroom. As a coach, you're never going to accomplish your goal without inspiring your pupils. Motivation is not a complicated concept, and it is not a difficult job to motivate the students. We live our lives with joy and happiness and with pain and sorrow, because we are inspired to move forward. Yes, often being ignored and disheartened in our lives, we avoid our hope of moving forward, but when human nature is encouraged, we start to think about moving forward again. Likewise, in most cases, without being inspired, the student loses hope to learn. That's why students need to be inspired.

A teacher can't be a good teacher unless he knows how to inspire a pupil. An excellent instructor is a person who knows the facts and techniques of how to create an active classroom, where the student can participate enthusiastically. In reality, without motivating your students, you won't be able to fulfill your sole responsibility.

There are a variety of approaches to inspire students in the classroom. Some of the best ideas for encouraging the students in the school are discussed below. In reality, these tips on motivating your students can help you to make your classroom more productive and creative.

Ensure Anxiety-Free Classroom

What do you know? Fear also inhibits learning outcomes. So, never seek to impose terror by enforcing punishments in your classroom. I have found that some of us, the teachers, are implementing extra assignments as punishment, because physical disciplines do not occur in teaching today as they did in the old and conventional period. Also, negative remarks often give rise to fear among students in the classroom. The fear in the classroom, whether it's for retribution or threatening comments, will never inspire the pupils. In reality, fear is an obstacle to participating successfully in the learning session. A student should never seek to take an inactive part in the classroom. That's why every teacher should maintain a fear-free class to inspire the students. So, never make negative statements and give burdening tasks as punishments.

Promote Their Ideas and Decisions

It is to promote creative learning in the classroom. Although offering assignments and coursework, giving them their freedom to choose the subject on their own. Your students are going to be inspired. You know, after all, human beings want gratitude. In reality, appreciation changes a lot of students' lives. Your students are unable to wait to take part in your next lecture. And if you enjoy fresh ideas, hundreds of excellent ideas will also be exposed to other students in your classroom.

So, always welcome new ideas to inspire your students.

Clarify the Objective

Every student likes clear instructions. Clarify each target goal to be accomplished at the beginning of the course.

Don't forget to mention the obstacles they might face during the session. Discuss possible antidotes about the challenges they might face.

They will, therefore, be inspired to address more problems, which will make the topic more accessible.

As a result, you will find that your classroom has become successful because your students are encouraged.

Improve the Environment of The Classroom

Don't always sit down to discuss the lesson. Move beside the students and think about the experience. Keep them out of your class occasionally.

Tell them to visit the library sometimes for research purposes.

The shift in the classroom environment stimulates the excitement of the learning brain, which is, in fact, a prerequisite for motivation.

Be A Good Listener

Listen carefully to what your students need to say. Appreciate their emotions and opinions. Take the right steps to solve the problems they talk about. Be a great listener, guys. They're going to start loving you when you listen to them with proper care. You will win their confidence. Now, is it not easy to inspire them? If you want your students to listen to you, you have to listen to them first.

Share Their Experience

Not all students can share their experience in the course of the class. Some of them will be occupied by reading books. As students discuss their lessons-related expertise, others may be inspired to participate actively. Prepare the lesson in such an inspiring way that all learners can engage actively in the lessons. In this situation, other students are often inspired to share their own experiences. You can, therefore, ensure that the classroom is successful.

Positive Competition

Constructive competition is, in essence, a useful strategy in the school. Ensure the rivalry is constructive. A good rivalry in group work motivates learners tremendously. We are also prepared to carry out community work, which will also bring significant benefits to their professional life. There is no doubt that healthy competition sparks excitement among the students in the classroom.

Know Your Student Well

You need to know your students well. You should also know their preferences, their dislikes, their effectiveness, and their lack of performance. When your students realize that you know them well, they will begin to like you and disclose their obstacles. This would make it easier for you to inspire your students on the right path. You will not be able to encourage them because you know them well.

Support Them and Give Them Responsibility

Give them the responsibility of the pupils. Assign them a class project. They're going to work with determination, for sure. In such a situation, individual students may also have to fulfill their obligations.

When you give them responsibilities, trust within themselves will grow, and they will begin to feel that they are valuable because they get value from you. They would then be inspired to engage more in the classroom. When you trust them, they will always trust you in return.

Show Your Enthusiasm

Convey your enthusiasm in the classroom during a lecture while meeting your duties. Share your excitement about their great success. Again, it shows an optimistic interest when a learner presents a new idea. Your expression of enthusiasm will encourage them.

Hold Your Record

Write a report for yourself. Write down every success of your pupils. If you find that a specific student is changing, speak to the student about the change. Show the student the records. Reward and support the student in front of the classroom. Even share the changes with your friends. If a student discovers that you're taking care of the student while you address from your record, the student is inspired.

Constructive Feedback

If a student is not doing well, including positive feedback. When necessary, offer a second chance. Be a friend and seek to understand the case of such a bad result. Encourage the student to inspire him/her to improve quickly next time as he/she did not understand how to do well in this subject with proper knowledge and technique. Your constructive reviews will change a lot of lives. Look closely at the worst-performing students in your school; you're going to get a lot of good qualities. Inform them of the beautiful qualities they possess. In reality, value them, which will inspire them significantly in return.

Real-Life Situation In the classroom

Relate your lesson plan to a real-life scenario. Make the lesson enjoyable with the fun of the game. Tell them a remarkable story with a mixture of humor. The reading thus makes it possible for the student to respond to his/her own experience. Let them also apply the lesson to their personal experience. Track it accurately. In reality, when you're dealing with your reading in real-life scenarios, students are encouraged to learn and attend your class.

Communicate with Your Parents and Guardians

Use the classroom to keep the parents and guardians in the loop. You should invite parents to sign up for a regular or weekly e-mail rundown of what's going on in their children's schools.

Emails contain the pending or unfinished work of a student, as well as updates and questions that you post in the class Stream.

Assigning Assignments to A Group of Students

Teachers may delegate work and post announcements to individual students or a group of students in a class.

This functionality helps teachers to distinguish instruction as required, as well as to promote collaborative group work.

Using the Classroom Mobile App Annotations

Students and teachers can use the Mobile Classroom on Android, iOS, and Chrome mobile devices.

You can provide input in real-time by annotating the student's work in the app. Students may also write down their tasks to convey an idea or concept more easily.

Explore the Integration of Classroom with Other Resources

Google Classroom uses an API to link and exchange knowledge with a variety of your favorite devices. Thousands of applications and websites are incorporated, like Pear Deck, Actively Read, Newsela, and many, many more.

Encourage Supervisors to Use Classroom Metrics

While this feature is for administrators — not teachers — it is still worth mentioning here. Administrators may use the Admin console to see statistics, such as how many classes have been created, how many posts have been posted. Teachers use the tool. Access to this knowledge will help customize teacher support.

CHAPTER 9:

Managing Google Classroom

The processes of assigning, gathering, marking, and returning student work can be simplified using Google Classroom. This saves time and removes those stacks of dreaded papers that need grading.

If you do not have a strategy for wading through it all, it can be just as intimidating and frustrating as conventional marking. Just like your grade book or textbook, Google Classroom is an instrument. How you make use of it will decide your performance.

Organizing Your Google Classroom Content

Organize your content by folders (subject, month, topics) so that the activities you want to delegate are easier to access. In Google Classroom, most of the items you delegate will come straight from your Google Drive. If you have a high content management program the next year will be a breeze with your next class.

Sharing Links and Resources

There are two ways of providing access to websites. You can create a link as an assignment and submit it to all your students. This also works in the case of videos that you want your students to watch for lessons or more information. If it's a link you're going to use frequently, then you might want to consider adding this to your class **About** section. This is a great place to incorporate website texting, learning tools, or websites your students need to use daily. Don't overuse this feature but putting some details here certainly saves your time.

Keep Your Google Classroom Feed Clean

The feed-in Google Classroom can get busy and confusing if you delegate several items every week. Deleting your older assignments that have been graded is a perfect way to keep the feed clean and easy to navigate. The exception to this will be assignments that you must delegate regularly, and which do not change much. These assignments may be reused and re-posted, with the option of reusing them the following year. One personal choice is how you handle the feed. If you want to reuse items, set them up in such a way that they can be edited easily and reused the first time you allocate them; this will save you time later. It is best not to return the assignment for younger students after you've marked it. This will mess up the feed of your students, and they do not understand why you give it back. They can see the grade, but it's vague, and they're not going to spend the time checking it. Returns can be reserved for those assignments which require only corrections. This way, your students will know that if an assignment is back in their feed and not marked "DONE," they need to improve the quality before sending it again.

Be a Good Coach

The teachers must be able to provide the students with positive feedbacks. Feedback can't only concentrate on the negative and positive aspects of student research, but can also give suggestions for change and provide incentives for change where permitted. Teachers will meet students on a one-to-one basis regularly to discuss the strengths and approaches to problems as they arise.

Strengthen Your Classroom and Don't Micromanage

A teacher needs to be able to balance the workload while also offering instruction and support, allowing students independence. Focus on the learning information that matters to a student, and step back from those that don't. Does this example need to be colored, or does it need to be done first for the student to excel in the lesson? If not, then let them decide what is right for them. Your aim is for them to obtain the information they need, and not to complete the research precisely as you want it!

Show Genuine Interest in the Success and Welfare of (Students)

A teacher has to know his students very well. They both have interests, impulses dislikes and tempers. Students have to feel comfortable in the classroom – not just the well-behaved ones! Some students are rough or have interests that vary greatly from those of their teachers. Still, showing interest in their lives is significant. Now, it must be stressing that a teacher needs to maintain a professional and authoritative relationship with all the students. Fortunately, this can be achieved in a friendly and open way!

Be Efficient and Concentrate on Performance

Keep the emphasis on what the team of students needs to achieve. Set goals they are aware of, and ensure that activities in the classroom push students towards those goals. Students enjoy fun games and events, so make sure what's prepared for them helps them gain the skills they need. It is not the duty of teachers to only spend the day with students, but also to train them according to clear expectations.

Be an Excellent Communicator and Talk to Your (Classroom)

Explain things simply and in many different ways. If a student doesn't understand, find new and creative ways to direct them to understand.

A teacher always needs to be approachable. Students need to know that they can comfortably ask questions and that their thoughts matter. Open a discussion in the classroom where you respect and listen to all opinions.

Be sure to set rules for respect because students may sometimes fail to think about their words before they talk. The open environment created will be of great value to the teacher's success in managing the classroom. Just like employees, when students know their thoughts matter, they're happier.

Help the Students Grow Humanly

Let the students learn how to set their own goals. Not just short-term goals, but goals that might take a while to attain. Then, direct them to approaches and tools which can enable them to achieve those goals if they need additional practice, provide it!

One day, these academic objectives will turn into the ability of each student to set career and personal goals.

Have a Clear Vision and Tactics for Your Student?

When something goes wrong, having clear goals and plans that are communicated and discussed with students will help keep things running as smoothly as possible. All students will know exactly what behavior is required of them, as well as have a good understanding of the rules of class and the implications of misconduct.

Consistency is the key! Teachers can change rules and procedures only when they need to. Frequent change may also lead students to feel that the rules are not as relevant as they ought to be.

This may even cause them to forget what is required of them *currently*.

Have Essential Technical Skills to Help Educate the (Classroom)

A teacher has to understand the work that is being offered. Not only that, but a teacher always needs to understand and predict the difficulties students face as they complete the assigned tasks. And, once those challenges come up, a teacher must be able to work with their students to overcome the obstacles they face. A teacher will sometimes find missing (still vital) skills. Many times, it may be as basic as a system that doesn't work the way it *should* and needs troubleshooting. Teachers must be prepared to roll up their sleeves and get to work with their students in any case!

How to Build Google Classroom Tasks

<u>Create an Assignment (Part 1)</u>

Within Google Classroom, assignments can be created and assigned to students, and there are a variety of useful choices for educators here. Here's what you have got to know:

- Open the class you wish to apply a job to.

- At the top of the list, click the tab **Classwork**

- Click the **Create** button and pick to add a task,

- Offer your assignment a title and include any more directions or explanations in the box below.

- Click on the date to select your assignment date and add time if you want to decide when it is due.

- By clicking on one of the icons next to the word **Assign**, choose the type of assignment you want to create. Your choices include uploading a file from your computer, inserting a Google Drive file, adding a YouTube video, or adding a link to a website.

- Press **Assign** to send your students the assignment.

If you want to give more than one class the same assignment, click on the class name in the top-left corner of the assignment window and pick all the classes you want to add the assignment to.

Create an Assignment (Part 2)

However, selecting the Drive tool in Google Classroom has an added value. This becomes obvious with the choices you get when selecting a file from the Drive.

1. Students may view the file: If you want all students to be able to access the file but not be able to change it in any way, choose this option. This is perfect for study guides and standardized handouts to which the entire class must have access.

2. Students can edit the file: If you want all students to be able to edit and work on the same paper, choose this. This would be perfect for a collaborative learning project where students work on different

slides in the same Google Presentation, or where they are collaboratively brainstorming ideas about something you want to discuss in your next learning.

3. Make a copy for each student: If you choose this option, Classroom will make every student in your class a copy of the original file and grant them editing rights to that file. The master copy of the instructor shall remain intact, and the students shall have no access to the original register. Choose that when you want a paper that has an essay question for students to work on easily, or a digital worksheet prototype where students can fill in the blanks with their own answers.

This level of automation was possible before Google Classroom but when incorporated into this new platform, it is much easier to handle.

Organize Assignments by Topic

A recent change to Google Classroom is its ability to organize theme-by-theme assignments. This helps you to group assignments together in the Classwork tab, by unit or form. Students and teachers will consider the task they are searching for more effectively. Follow the instructions below to create topics.

- Navigate to your class.

- Click on the tab **Classwork**.

- Click on the button **Create.**

- Select **Topic**.

- Name your topic and click **Add**.

You can add new assignments to a topic from the creation screen for the assignment. Simply click the drop-down box next to **Subject** before allocating it. If you have already generated assignments that need to be transferred to a topic, follow these steps.

- Click on the **Classwork** tab.

- Hover over the assignment you want to move with your mouse.

- Click the three-dotted button.

- Choose **Edit.**

- Look for the drop-down box next to **Topic.**

- Click the drop-down menu and choose the topic you want to move it to.

How Students Complete Their Assignments and Send Them

A more convenient approach, however, is to press the **Menu** button in the screen's top-left corner and pick **To-do** from the pop-up display.

Clicking on one of those assignments will open the student's related tab. If it is a Google Drive file, in the top right-hand corner next to the **Sharing** button, an additional button is attached to the toolbar. This button is labelled **Turn it in**. Clicking on it submits their assignment to the instructor.

Grading and Returning Assignments to Students

Teachers will consider a variety of different ways to search for pupils. Perhaps the most effective method, however, is to join the class that you are involved in grading and click on the assigned name from the Stream view.

- If you notice that assignments get lost between student conversations, look at the sidebar at the top left of the Stream view and you will see the **Coming Assignments** box. Tap on the assignment to be evaluated, and follow the instructions below:

- Click on the name of the student who submitted an assignment you would like to rate.

- Use the commenting feature in Drive to leave comprehensive feedback on particular parts of the student submission when the document opens. When you're done, shut down the folder. All modifications are automatically saved.

- Click to the right of the name of the student (where it says **No grade)** when you return to Classroom, and enter a point-based grade for the assignment.

- Check the box next to the student you have just graded. Then, click the **Return** button to save the grade and inform the student that their paper has been graded.

- Add any additional input in the pop-up box, then click on **Return Assignment**.

CHAPTER 10:

E-learning Limitations

W hy do you want to be part of such a classroom network where you can connect with the learners, have them give positive input anytime they want it, and optimize the exchange of documents including assignments in the classroom?

This is what Google Classroom is doing; it is indeed Google's groundbreaking contribution to online learning as well as to the education management program industry.

It intends to make classrooms worldwide paperless, and also more productive. Google Classroom becomes accessible via Google Applications for education since it is actually only intended for academic entities, rather than for corporate training.

This chapter will present an analysis of Google Classroom by listing a few possible drawbacks along with solutions, to help you determine if Google Classroom is appropriate for the online courses, as there are always some limitations associated with different platforms. This chapter will highlight those issues and will explain how those issues could be tackled.

Virtual Education and its Limitations

While advancement is generally seen as a positive thing, there are many clear technical drawbacks in Classroom. EdTech isn't really a silver bullet for any situation through distraction to decreased face time. That being said, with some understanding, most disruptions can be tackled, such as the shockingly old-school mindset that deals with technical inequalities. So, move on in Classroom for some of the technical drawbacks. There is no lack of digital technologies from applications or e-textbooks up to organizational tools and "game elements." Education technology tools could make lessons increasingly engaging and usable for technically-educated students, and they can test teachers alike and contribute to optimal student outcomes. How will teachers make the most of the technology without losing effectiveness or commitment? Below are the technology drawbacks within Classroom, as well as how the students can get around them.

It Invites Distractions

Smartphones have a bad impression in classrooms and there have been many incidents in schools to ban them. Evidence shows that while students invested 42 percent of the time in a classroom on the devices, it was for email, tweeting, or otherwise browsing social media instead of lessons. Nonetheless, it is unlikely that bans on gadgets like smartphones will succeed because students eventually get by them. Those very bans would also be despised by learners who see the utilization of technology as a question of individual autonomy which should be regulated only when it diverts other learners. Teachers could still enable students to learn better methods of self-control to assist them to enforce their use of gadgets. A study shows that quality teaching methods that encourage student engagement get less technology usage off-task.

Needs Monitoring and Preparation

EdTech 's rise means teachers must be successful at a computer or a tech platform to be effective in teaching. Statistics indicate that 75% of teachers say that the internet or other digital technologies have brought new requirements to their daily lives. Therefore, they have significantly expanded the amount of information and expertise they need to be informed about, with almost half reporting that their workload is enlarged.

Leads to Disparity in Technology

Technology disparity relates to how many students have access to the appropriate technology. The disparities in access among school districts can be seen, with more wealthy districts provided more funding. It could also apply to disparities between students in the same facility, where learners from more affluent families have better access. The recent study reveals that although 84% of teenagers use the smartphone, the remaining do not. The target is to hit 16%. Tech inequality frequently applies to education and school policy decisions. The aforementioned report also points out this. However,

75% of teachers employed in affluent districts believed the schools offered enough preparation, just half of the teachers of low-income localities approved. Approximately 40% of teachers from economically deprived areas perceived the schools a little behind the technical innovation curve.

Costing Money

Everything about this world will change, so it is very costly to purchase cutting-edge technology for schools. Although there is no option to prevent spending resources modifying a class, by deploying tools with greater longevity but also decreased servicing, it is at minimum determining optimal the cumulative cost with respect to ownership.

Technology from higher operating costs will potentially end up saving money for the school, since it has fewer challenges and has less maintenance while still being smooth in use. Educational institutions need to carefully evaluate TCO before making technology acquisitions.

In addition, any use of tech should never be limited to students, but in reality, it has been used to optimize administrative processes, minimize costs, improve efficiency, and reduce wasted time performing administrative duties. In context, cloud computing offers schools considerable chances of saving money. Shifting to a virtual curriculum removes any need to update obsolete textbooks constantly.

Less Time in Sight

Hardly any amount of technology can substitute skilled, motivated teachers in a classroom. While the saying goes, every teacher who could be substituted by a tech tool certainly deserves replacement. Technology is not the answer for maintaining a safe, vigorous educational environment, it is just a pedagogical resource that is just as useful as the teacher who possesses it. In reality, while digital technology spends billions, nations that really do not deploy technology often have higher learning results compared to nations that invest extensively.

CHAPTER 11:

Additional Extensions for Google Classroom

Teachers are always looking for more effective ways to complete the work, but also exciting ways to engage the learning process with their students. Whether you are using a Chromebook on your PC/Mac or are just using Google Chrome, there are useful tools right at your fingertips which you might even not know exist.

These are Google extensions for teachers that can be easily installed in the Chrome browser and then accessed by clicking a button.

Pocket

Pocket is an extension that helps you to store later posts, images, and sites that you may like to check. Whenever you visit a video or a website that you'd like to recall after downloading Pocket, you only need to click on the extension in Chrome and the Pocket will transfer it to you.

When you sign into Wallet, you would be able to see all the pages, photos, and documents you saved. It is a great resource to keep track of the items you need for lessons in the future for career development.

Pear Deck

Pear Deck is an immersive tool for creating presentations. You may open a display of Google Slides once enabled and use the Pear Deck to attach questions to every slide. There may be several responses, brief answers, or questions. Students must sign in to your presentation, which will appear on their devices.

The questions that you have added should show on will student screen as you proceed through your presentation to offer them a chance to answer. You will see what every student reacts to, but you may also post their responses to the class privately so that they can view how others react. The very next question you have used comes up for students as you pass on to the next screen. Ultimately, you may save and upload student comments to Google Sheets and see how students react, and then decide a plan of action with the data you obtain later.

Checkmark

Checkmark is an enhancement that enables you to give quick reviews in Google Docs on a student's article. Rather than typing out any remarks you wish to add, you can set up any comments you make on student articles, such as "new paragraph," "run-on," or "comma mistake," and easily paste the message. Upon downloading and launching the extension all you must do is open your student file and then highlight a section of the file. A small box will then show up with the choices for responses, pick the correct response and it will be inserted automatically. If you like, you do have the right to include further notes; Checkmark can assist you with correct input in grading the papers quickly.

Auto Text Expander

Auto Text Expander helps you to type in emails via a shortcut for your long messages. For example, you might usually type "Thanks for your email" many times in response to inquiries from parents or students about the grade assigned. You can make a shortcut using Auto Text Expander, such as "ty," which will immediately insert the text you want. You may set up various self-contained shortcuts centered on bits of text that you always use. It will help you compose emails quickly and react to emails you get.

Doctopus and Goobric work well, and if you use Google Classroom they work particularly well. Doctopus pulls in Google Classroom essays and assignments with links to every individual assignment. Goobric lets you create a rubric with which each document can be opened. You may build your own rubrics or use models from Goobric. When you simultaneously open a student's assignment and also Goobric, Goobric opens in a side panel. Here, you can press on the boxes in the rubric you choose to rate and give feedback. Goobric sums it up and offers an average ranking, so it will send the student an email message that they are marked and ready to display their assignment. These two extensions will help streamline the input on research for the students.

Screencastify

Screencastify is an app that allows you to make a video of something on your screen. It's interesting because, instead of making PDF copies of anything you choose to use in your video, you can have an article and website accessible on your laptop. After Screencastify has been enabled and accessed, you can opt to film the open window, the whole screen, or even attach the camera in the bottom corner to capture yourself. When the recording is started, you will use the mouse to highlight and write numerous portions with the computer. Save the video to Google Drive, so students and workers will share it with you. This is particularly useful for e-learning lessons on the LMS, or for checking lessons.

Hopefully, such Google Chrome teacher extensions will help you communicate and grade more effectively.

A Few More Efficient Google Chrome Extensions For Online Distance Learning

Emoji Keyboard

Use this to bring visual value to subjects on Google Classroom. You can navigate the entire emoji library in your window bar from an icon, by utilizing the Emoji keyboard feature. When you ask what distance-learning emojis have to offer the world, check it out. Adding emojis to items like homework instructions and subjects specific to Google Classroom not only creates visual interest, but can also greatly boost readability. Often, emojis are particularly useful as bullet point symbols and to give focus on essential information.

Custom Cursor

Adjust the default mouse cursor to a range of colors and designs. Custom Cursor is a very fun extension that replaces your default cursor with one in a variety of styles and colors. Although it seems like a random as well as unnecessary tool, things like screen recordings and demonstrations are actually helpful. By default, the mouse pointers are comparatively small and non-descriptive, so swapping them out can help students track your moves easily in an online video because they can follow something a little more noticeable.

Bitmoji

In the greater scheme of things, Bitmoji may sound like another unnecessary addition, but introducing a bit of personalization to the online learning space may be helpful to both students and teachers. With your Bitmoji Chrome extension, adding your Bitmoji to your daily instructional materials is just one simple drag-and-drop action. You can use it to create a Google Meet, virtual Bitmoji scene, or updated Google Classroom banner. Another enjoyable way to use the Bitmoji is to make Bitmoji stickers digitally in Google Drawings, which can then be added in Google Classroom or the Seesaw to student research.

Mote

Record and then send voice comments to Google Docs, Sheets, and Slides, using the Chrome extension commented on by Mote's voice. If you're searching for a fast way to give students verbal input, Mote's your new MVP. Mote is an extension of a voice recording that works smoothly and continuously in Google Documents, Sheets, and slides. Teachers can submit voice feedback to the students instantly and conveniently using the native message function of Google. To make a comment, simply highlight the text, then click the Mote icon which appears on the side of the comment box. Students can listen to your audio comment by clicking on the recording link that will be posted with your comments.

Some Other Significant Extensions For Google Chrome

There are so many good extensions to Chrome that listing all of them will be difficult. With that, some extensions are a must-have, because they provide much-needed features, better protection, and improve Chrome's performance.

Those are the following:

Extensity

Extensity is the extension manager which enables you to swiftly allow and disable the extensions when required. Usually, you don't want to add so many extensions, particularly those you don't need because they increase the memory Chrome uses. With Extensity, when you need them, you can easily activate extensions, and uninstall them when you don't.

Chrome New Window Focus

The extension of New Window Focus for Chrome has been trying to fix a bug that has been present in Chrome for several years: whenever any new window on Chrome is opened, it sometimes does not get focused, and it is left behind the other windows. This extension will attempt to force any recently created window into focus.

HTTPS Everywhere

HTTPS Everywhere is also an extension generated by the EFF and Tor Project that changes thousands of pages automatically from vulnerable HTTP to HTTPS. It will shield you from certain monitoring and hijacking accounts, and from other types of censorship.

Last Pass is a Free Password Manager

Last Pass is a password manager that allows you to use very unique passwords on every website you visit, without needing to remember any of them. With the number of pages hacked, it is crucial that everybody uses complex and special passwords for each site visited by them. One such extension makes it much easier to achieve that process.

The Great Suspender

Great Suspender is often a light-weight extension for Chrome which helps to reduce the memory footprint of Chrome for users who like to have so many browser tabs at the same time. This extension would unload every window automatically while maintaining its favicon & title document. You can restore a tab by clicking on the page anywhere it's required. This decreases the number of DOM components on the website, which guarantees that there are no memory leaks or an excessive JavaScript.

Authy

The Authy extension allows codes necessary for two-factor authentication to be simply produced.

Adblock Plus

Adblock Plus is an ad blocker which often assists websites by not preventing any unobtrusive advertising.

Lazarus, Which Provides Recovery

One of the most irritating situations is when you fill a long questionnaire and either mistakenly shut the application window or the system fails before you can register it. Lazarus is an extension to Chrome that records what users type in forms, so you can get it back later.

Crypt Up that Encrypt Gmail

Crypt Up makes it extremely simple to send authenticated PGP emails via Gmail. It is a perfect alternative to use for someone who is concerned about someone spying on their messages but doesn't want to struggle with the hassle of setting up a PGP.

CHAPTER 12:

Hidden Features of Google Classroom

Did you recognize some hidden features inside Google Classroom you may enjoy? This chapter will pass over the top five ones, why they matter, and how you may use them to improve your experience.

Templates

If you're an instructor, this is certainly a good feature to have. While it could now not be a hidden function, it's frequently entirely not noted.

If you're searching for a perfect template to reveal notes, a letter, or even formalize any record, that is something that you need to consider. It is also exact for college students, specifically, if they generally tend to have unfinished class projects they want a reminder to finish.

For example, if they are to write a resume, it's much easier to do it with this template than using a generic file from Google Docs.

This is a terrific function that may be located on the homepage of Google Docs, and you may observe the many options.

The Hidden Assignment Calendar

This part is an assignment calendar that's used to hold both college students and instructors working together. Every time instructors create questions, there are due dates connected to it, and you could see this right away in the calendar of Google Classroom. To locate it, go to the **Menu** and press the location that announces the schedule. Once it shows, you can see all of the work assigned to your class and whatever else that is due soon. Teachers also get the G Suite calendar, that can be used to position assignments in too, and you could get entry (without delay) to add distinct events. For example, discipline trips, tutoring, or maybe meetings can be put in. You can also add general faculty occasions too, so every unmarried student is on the right track. It helps to keep everybody together.

Research Tool

This tool is a device for the people using Google Docs who want to have some online studies delivered to their tasks. It's, in reality, brilliant and simple, given that it permits you to refer to images and reviews without leaving your file. It's an underrated and regularly left-out feature, but it's been there; you just likely didn't understand it. You can either open it from the **Equipment** section or adequately click on a word to studies. Or you can press Control + Alt + Shift, and then I. You are then given an entire group of topics associated with what you searched for, whether they are popular Wikipedia articles, snapshots, or scholarly articles. Then, you may choose the content, and position it in your file, and additionally cite it easily. It's an underrated device that's a godsend for many folks who do studies and papers, given that it can be used the right way and makes your learning easier. It's a hidden feature of Google Classroom that allows the classroom to enjoy being even higher for each student and instructors.

Copy Header

If you're creating a Google websites page together with a scholar website, this is a wonderful device that can be used to help improve the navigation of this site. Every time you create a new page, you're given a blank header, but some instructors need to use a similar heading, or maybe the identical one for every single web page they have. If you need to do this, the first thing to do is click the webpage that has the banner to reuse. From there, press the icon with a plus, and then pick the option. Then add to the new page, which reasons it to be copied over again. It's a hidden function for teachers who are using Google websites within their Google Classroom software, and it may make a massive difference if you want to save a little bit of time and make your life simpler.

Filtering Searches

This filter is a hiding location that's in plain sight. At the very top of the Drive, you'll see an arrow that is going down along the edge. Once you click on it, you'll accept many extraordinary seek alternatives, to filter out one of a kind search results. This is a lifesaver for teachers because if you were given a ton of different tasks which might be taking place down the pipeline, you need to be able to get to all of the files. If you have a vast library as a scholar, that is an excellent manner to slender down the results. You can clear it out using the exceptional record types, the names of the files, and even the date they have been modified by user as well. For data shared, you could filter it out and with the aid of the persons you've shared the report with, too. You also can utilize the action item that includes this, or any hints you'd love to do to the record. It's a terrific way to help you in organizing your Drive, and for each college students and instructors who use Google Classroom, it saves loads of time. After all, if you're an instructor who teaches multiple sections or covers quite a few route contents, it could be a nightmare to keep up with it all; however, this will make your life less difficult in the long run.

These capabilities are, in a few instances, hidden in plain sight; however, a number of them are underrated tools that could facilitate you. For the average instructor or pupil, those various capabilities could make a world of a difference in your potential to use Google Classroom, so it's essential to make certain that you use these extraordinary capabilities because they can assist and improve your life.

CHAPTER 13:

Working with Google Classroom

How to Interact with Your Students

Post Announcements to Your Trainees

You can post statements to your class on the **Stream** page. Announcements are posts with no assignments. Use them to offer notices to your trainees. Statements appearing on the **Stream** page in chronological order. If you desire, you can move an older post to the top.

Students get an email for each announcement; however, they can turn off the e-mail alert feature.

You can draft and arrange statements, and also control who comments or responds to posts. For details on commenting, see **Set Class Approvals**.

You can post announcements to one or more classes, or pick students in a class. You can likewise add tools.

Post an announcement

1. Go to *classroom.google.com*.

2. Click on the class.

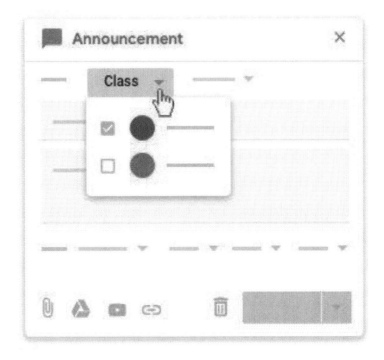

3. On the **Stream** page, click **Share something with your class**.

4. Enter your statement and click **Post**.

Keep in mind that as you type your announcement, Classroom immediately waits and puts a draft in **Saved statements** at the top of the **Stream**.

The announcement to multiple classes goes to all students in those classes.

Next to **For**, click on the **Down** arrow. Pick the classes you desire.

Post to Private Students

Unless you're publishing to multiple classes, you can publish an announcement to specific students (but not more than 100).

1. Click **All pupils** again to deselect students.

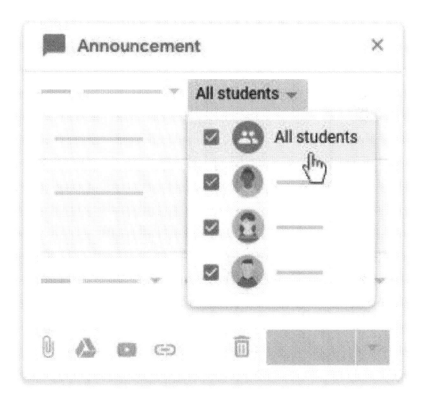

2. To choose a trainee, click on their name.

On the **Stream** page, you can see the number of trainees the statement was posted to.

3. To see the trainees' names, on the announcement, click the number of trainees (optional).

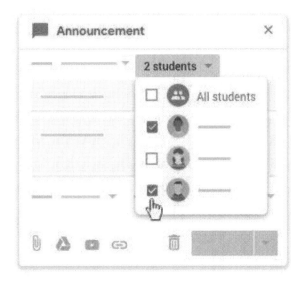

Add a remark to a published announcement

1. Go to *classroom.google.com*.

2. Click on the class.

3. On the **Stream** page, find the posted statement and click **Add class remark**.

4. Click and post a comment.

Delete A Statement

1. Go to *classroom.google.com*.

2. Choose the relevant alternative:

For a posted statement:

a) On the **Stream** page, next to the statement, click **More** > **Delete**.

b) To verify, click **Delete** once again.

For a scheduled or draft statement:

a) At the uppermost part of the **Stream** page, select **Saved statements**.

b) Besides the statement, click **Remove** > **Delete**.

Move an Announcement to The Top

You can move a statement or any other post to the top of the **Stream**.

1. Go to *classroom.google.com.*

2. Click on the class.

3. On the **Stream** page, click **Move to top** on the statement.

Email Your Trainees

You can email a trainee, a group of students, or a whole class.

To email trainees, Gmail should be switched on for you and your students.

For your students to send out an e-mail in Classroom, the Gmail and Directory services must be switched on for trainees.

For help, call your G Suite administrator.

Tips for Sending Emails To Your Classes

You can email approximately 100 recipients simultaneously. If a class has more than 100 trainees, you're required to email some trainees initially and after that send out the message once again to the remaining students.

You can only email one class at a time

To send out a message to multiple classes at the same time, post an announcement to multiple classes.

How to Send out an Email:

1. Go to *classroom.google.com*.

2. Click your class.

3. At the top, click on **People**.

4. Pick an alternative:

Email one student: Next to the trainee's name, click **More Email** trainee.

Email numerous students: Check the box beside each student's name. At the top, click **Actions Email**.

Email the entire class: Next to **Actions**, inspect the box. Click **Actions** > **Email**.

Keep in mind that when you email multiple students, the default setting includes the addresses to the *Bcc* field. You can move trainees' addresses to the *To* or *Cc* fields.

5. Go into a topic for your message.

6. To connect links, files, or photos to your message, go to **Send attachments** with your Gmail message (optional).

7. Enter your message and click **Send**.

View an e-mail

1. Go to *classroom.google.com*.

2. At the top, click on the **App Launcher Gmail**.

Share to Classroom from A Mobile Phone

You can share links, videos, images, and Google Drive items to Classroom on your gadget.

1. On the site, image, link, or video, tap **Share Classroom**.

2. By default, the last active class is chosen. To alter the class, tap **Next**, then select another class.

3. Tap the kind of post you want to use.

4. Complete the question, announcement, or assignment, and tap **Post**.

I do not see the **Share to Classroom** icon.

If you do not see **Share to Classroom**, you can still share the webpage using these alternatives:

Add the URL to a question, statement, or task.

Use the **Share a web page** with your class Chrome extension. Site owners include the Share to Classroom extension, so if the icon is missing, it implies that the site owner hasn't added it to their site.

To add **Share to Classroom** to a website:

Talk to the individual who owns the site.

Before you start using Google Classroom, make sure that you have a Google account, or have one created for you.

How to Download Grades to Google Sheets

You can export the students' scores in a Comma Separated Values (CSV) file format to Google Sheets. This allows the teacher to study student performance closely. With Google Sheets, you can further analyze the data to find information, such as average scores and so on.

Here is how to go about doing this:

Go to your class on Google Classroom.

At the top of the screen, select **Classwork**.

Next, click on the assignment whose scores you wish to export.

Click on **View Assignment**.

The **Student Work** page will be displayed. On that page, select **Settings**.

Click on **Copy All Grades to Google Sheets**. A spreadsheet containing the grades will be created in Google Sheets.

Rubric

Here is how to import rubrics other teachers share with you.

On your Google Classroom home page, click **Classwork.**

Select **Create.**

Click **Assignment**, and then enter a title for the assignment.

Click **Add Rubric**.

Select **Import from Sheets.** The folder containing imported sheets will be opened.

Select the rubric you wish to import and click **Add**.

Click **Save**.

How to Schedule Events, Set Due Dates, And Manage Assignments

Teachers can share a Classroom calendar and Google Calendar with students and fellow teachers. With the Classroom calendar, you can view classwork due dates and all your assignments. With Google Calendar, you can view and add classwork due dates, view class events, view personal reminders, and add events.

Working with Appointment Calendars

Calendars help you view upcoming events and soon-to-be-due assignments.

To view due dates on your Classroom calendar:

Sign in to the class.

Click on **Menu** (it is the three-lined button at the top-left corner).

Click on **Calendar.**

There will be several options available. Choose the option that aligns with what you want to do.

To check past events, assignments, and upcoming assignments, click on the **Back/Next** arrows.

To view assignments given for all classes, click on the **All Classes** option.

To view assignments given in one particular class, click on **All Classes** to reveal a dropdown menu. Select the class from the options displayed.

You can open and view assignments directly from the Calendar. Simply click on the assignment or question.

To view items and due dates on your calendar:

Login to *classroom.google.com.*

At the top of the screen, click on **Menu** (three-lined button).

Click **Calendar**.

You can choose to see past or future work, assignments for all classes, and assignments for one class. To see past or future work, click **Back** or **Next**. To view assignments for all your classes, select **All classes**.

To view assignments for one class, tap **All classes**, and then select the class you want.

128 | P a g .

Adding an Event to Google Calendar

You can add events, invite classmates, and add other activities to your Google Calendar. To do so:

Sign in to *classroom.google.com.*

Select **Class > Classwork.**

Select **Google Calendar.**

Go to **Create an event.**

How to Create an Assignment

Sign in to *classroom.google.com.*

Tap the class. At the bottom of the screen, click **Create assignment.**

Input the title and fill out other instructions.

How to Change an Assignment Due Date

By default, your assignment is scheduled for the next day after creating it. However, it is still subject to change. To change it:

Click on the **Down** arrow next to **Due tomorrow.**

Tap the date and select your date. If you wish to set a due time, select **Time** and type the time.

If you also want to create an assignment without a due date, tap **Due Date** and click **Remove** next to the date.

Conclusion

L earning is a method that lasts for life. Nothing is more suitable than the proverb that refers to instructors and educators everywhere in the world as a traditional annual teacher attend continuing training courses. The goal is to make certain that their statistics are not infiltrated by obsolescence. Additionally, training courses continue to provide instructors with methodologies that help students in diverse and creative styles of learning. The upside for teachers is to share satisfactory practices and have a better control on students and classroom behaviors.

Continual training is offered to make sure teachers are at the vanguard of the new educational tendencies regarding methodologies and technologies. Continued trainer training may be likened to a bridge linking in-field exceptional practices of individuals and groups. Continued education is meant to hold instructors up-to-date and to find music their coaching processes, in an effort to obtain significant results from students.

Continual training commonly covers self-serving slides or displays and different similar resources that educators needed simply to click and complete. To take a look at their efficacy has been no follow-up, partnership, or discussion. In current years, however, this has changed, with persevering schooling sources becoming highly complete and reliable. Consequently, today's sources are not the most effective to encompass self-learning. However, they investigate and calculate efficacy via diverse touchpoints, which includes supplementary learning materials, participating with friends and experts, completing assignments, and discussions on relevant topics within exact timeframes. Examples of this online technology mixed with offline studying are LearnPort from Michigan and Teacher's Line from PBS. The emphasis isn't always most effective on isolated eLearning. Actively enticing groups through online and offline forums via the use of the brand-new net technologies around the county and across the world is important. Web 2.0 sources, together with Facebook, Wikis, Podcasts, Skype, Moodle, Ning, Flat Classroom, and Google Docs, are now used more regularly in contemporary times. Such social networking resources are beneficial to teachers and educators in their professional development. They help do away with boundaries like territorial obstacles and time zones. Additional continuing training applications for instructors consist of in-house lectures, webinars, workshops, and conferences, alongside courses supplied in university campuses and college districts. Continue teaching courses that concentrate on particular subjects of coaching consisting of arithmetic and physics to improve their methodologies of teaching. The above, additionally, consists of the brand-new improvements which may be carried out into the classrooms. An example of this is virtual classrooms. Also, they'll provide instructors with improved abilities in schoolroom control and related tasks as well.

Printed in Great Britain
by Amazon